Indonesian Recipes

Discover the Taste of In

BY

Stephanie Sharp

WWWWWWWWWWWWWWWWWWWWWWWWWWWWWWWW

License Notes

wwwwwwwwwwwwwwwwwwwwwwwwwwwwwwwwwwww

Table of Contents

Introduction

People of Indonesia love their culture and they showcase their culture with their food. Whatever they are, they will assemble it in their dining table. There are certain foods or certain ingredients that are more commonly used in Indonesia. People there love spicy food. They use red chilies in abundance. They love to use shrimp paste and peanut butter in most of their dishes. The uses whole peanuts and crushed peanuts, peanut paste in their food. There is a classic peanut dipping sauce, to die for. Check the recipe and try making it yourself.

They love tofu and tempeh. You will see the use of these vegetarian items quite often. They also love coconut and coconut milk is used quite often in their curries and desserts. They love to incorporate eggs in their meals too.

They endorse a good healthy eating habit. Therefore, they try to add herbs and spices to their food. Spices like nutmeg, cinnamon, cardamom, bay leaf, and clove are seen. They are to combine one key ingredient with a minor ingredient to make a dish unique. Often time meat is combined with vegetables to give it a healthy kick.

You will also find their traditional dessert in this book. Try these 30 Indonesian recipes and plunge into their spice world.

Recipes

Turmeric Beef and Celery Curry

Indo people love their spices. You will see plenty of red chilies in their cooking. Beef do taste better when it is properly spiced. The celery in this dish gives the dish a soft texture.

Serving Size: 4

Cooking Time: 50 Minutes

Ingredients:

- 2 lb. beef
- 5 shallots, chopped
- 2 small red chilies, chopped
- 1 cup diced celery
- 1 tbsp finely grated ginger
- 6 cashew nuts
- 2 tbsp oil
- 1 tbsp soy sauce
- 1 tomato, roughly chopped
- 1 tsp turmeric
- 2 tsp red chili powder
- 1 tsp cumin

Instructions:

Cut the beef into medium pieces.

In a large pan, heat the oil.

Sear the beef for 5 minutes. Add the turmeric, cumin, red chili powder, grated ginger, shallots and mix well.

Cover and cook on high heat for 20 minutes.

Add the red chilies, celery, tomato, soy sauce and mix well.

Cover and cook for another 20 minutes.

Add the cashew nuts on top before serving.

Simple Egg Nasi Goreng

Nasi goreng is one of the most famous dishes out there in Indonesia. This is a simple egg fried rice recipe that anyone can make at home.

Serving Size: 4

Cooking Time: 35 Minutes

Ingredients:

- 2 lb. rice
- 4 eggs
- 1 cucumber, thinly slices, to serve
- 2 tbsp soy sauce
- 2 tbsp tomato sauce
- Salt and pepper to taste
- 2 tbsp oil
- 2 garlic cloves, minced

For the Spice Paste:

- 2 small shallots, chopped
- 3 garlic cloves
- 1 green chili,
- 1/2 teaspoon shrimp paste

Instructions:

First of all combine all the spice paste ingredients in a blender.

Blend until smooth. Set aside for now.

In a pot add the rice with salted boiling water. Cook for 10 minutes.

Drain well and rinse the rice properly. In a wok heat the oil with medium flame.

Add the minced garlic and toss for 1 minute. Add the spice paste and 2 tbsp of water.

Stir continuously for 1 minute. Add 3 of the eggs and scramble them properly.

Add the cooked rice and toss for 1 minute.

Add the soy sauce, tomato sauce, salt, pepper, and mix well. Stir for 5 minutes and take off the heat. In another pan fry an egg and add on top of the rice. Serve hot with slices cucumber on the side.

Indonesian-style chicken salad

Indonesians love their Chicken salad. The dressing of the dish is light and flavorful, and the crunchiness of the peanuts is something to remember.

Serving Size: 2

Cooking Time: 25 Minutes

Ingredients:

- 2 chicken breasts
- 1 sweet potato, cut into wedges
- 2 carrot, cut into thin slices
- 1 cup fresh mint leaves
- ½ cup toasted peanuts
- ½ cup spring onion, sliced
- Fresh parsley, chopped
- 2 teaspoons soy sauce
- 2 cucumber, chopped
- 1 garlic clove, crushed
- Salt and pepper to taste
- 1/2 teaspoon brown sugar
- 1 tbsp canola oil
- 1 tablespoon coconut oil

Instructions:

Combine the soy sauce, salt, pepper, brown sugar and coconut oil in a bowl. Mix well and set aside for now.

In a pan, add the canola oil and fry the sweet potato wedges until golden brown. Transfer to a bowl.

Add the chicken breasts and sprinkle some salt and pepper.

Fry for 4 minutes on each side. Transfer to a plate. Cut into slices.

Add to the mixing bowl. Add the cucumber, carrot, spring onion, mint leaves, parsley, and garlic.

Toss well and add the dressing. Add the toasted peanuts and mix well.

Serve fresh.

Cucumber Salad with Grills Chicken

Grilled chicken tastes great but when you add Indonesian Spice blend to it, it gets elevated and becomes irresistible. The fresh salad also complements the chicken.

Serving Size: 4

Cooking Time: 10 Minutes

Ingredients:

For the salad:

- 2 cucumbers cut into cubes
- 2 tomatoes, chopped
- 1 cup shredded cabbage
- ½ cup toasted peanuts
- ½ cup shredded carrots
- 4 tbsp fresh basil leaves
- 2 tbsp lemon juice
- Salt and pepper to taste

For the chicken:

- 4 chicken pieces
- Salt and pepper to taste
- 2 red chilies
- 1 dried red chili
- 1 tsp turmeric
- 2 tbsp coconut paste
- 1 tsp coconut oil
- 2 tbsp garlic paste
- 2 inch ginger root, minced
- 1 tsp lemon juice

- 1 tbsp shrimp paste

Instructions:

Combine the lemon juice, shrimp paste, ginger, garlic paste, coconut paste, turmeric, salt, pepper, red chilies, and dried chili in a blender.

Blend into a smooth paste. Marinate the chicken pieces with the mixture.

Let it sit for 2 hours. Add the oil to the grilling pan.

Then grill the chicken for 5 minutes on each side.

In another bowl, combine the tomatoes, cabbage, carrots, basil leaves, and cucumbers.

Add the toasted peanuts, lemon juice, salt, and pepper.

Toss well and mix everything. Serve.

Shrimp Nasi goreng

Nasi Goreng is the number one staple in the Indonesian Cuisine. This is a shrimp fried rice with vegetables served with freshly sliced cucumbers and tomatoes.

Serving Size: 4

Cooking Time: 35 Minutes

Ingredients:

- 2 cup long-grain rice
- 1 cup shrimp, deveined, peeled
- ½ cup green beans, cut in half
- 2 onion, chopped
- 2 chicken breasts, diced
- 4 garlic cloves, sliced
- Pepper to taste
- 1 red chili, deseeded, chopped
- 4 large eggs, beaten
- 3 tbsp vegetable oil
- 1 tbsp lemon juice
- 2 tbsp soy sauce
- Salt to taste
- Cucumber slices to serve
- Tomato slices to serve

Instructions:

Soak the rice for 30 minutes in the water. Drain and wash well.

Add to a pot with salted water. Bring it to boil. Cook for 10 minutes.

Drain and rinse off well. Set aside for now.

In a wok, heat the vegetable oil. Fry the onion for 1 minute.

Add the garlic and toss for 1 minute. Add the chicken pieces and cook for 5 minutes. Add the eggs and scramble them finely.

Add the red chili, shrimp and green beans.

Add salt, pepper, soy sauce, lemon juice and toss for 5 minutes.

Add the rice and then cook for another 5 minutes.

Serve hot with cucumbers and tomatoes.

Left-over Turkey Fried Rice

Indonesians love nasi goreng so much that whenever there is a leftover meat, they make fried rice with it. Traditionally it is served with fried egg on top and cucumber slices on the side. This recipe is made using left-over turkey. Feel free to use any meats of your choices.

Serving Size: 2

Cooking Time: 25 Minutes

Ingredients:

- 1 cup long grain rice
- 1 cup leftover turkey, shredded
- 1 egg
- 1/3 cup vegetable oil
- 1 inch ginger root, thinly sliced
- 2 eggs, whisked
- 1 red onion, chopped
- 3 garlic cloves, sliced
- 1 red chili, finely sliced
- 1 tbsp soy sauce
- 1 tbsp lemon juice
- 1 tsp mixed herbs
- Cucumber slices to serve
- Coriander leaves to serve

Instructions:

Cook the rice in a pot with the salted water for 10 minutes. Drain and set aside for now.

In a pan, add the oil. Fry the garlic with the onion for 2 minutes.

Add the eggs and scramble them. Add the turkey and toss for 2 minutes.

Add the red chili, lemon juice, ginger, soy sauce, and mixed herbs. Add salt, pepper and mix well.

Add the cooked rice and toss for 5 minutes.

In another pan fry the egg. Add on top of the rice.

Add the cucumber slices and coriander leaves on top and serve hot.

Gado gado

Gado gado is a popular Indonesian Salad recipe. This one contains crispy fried tofu, boiled egg and few fruits and vegetables.

Serving Size: 4

Cooking Time: 10 Minutes

Ingredients:

- 2 cup charlotte potatoes
- 1 cup firm tofu, cubed
- 1 cup shredded cabbage
- 1 tbsp butter
- 2 eggs
- ½ cup cherry tomatoes, chopped
- ½ cup baby radish cut in half
- 2 garlic cloves, crushed
- Salt and pepper to taste
- 1 tsp chili flakes
- 2 tbsp soy sauce
- 2 tbsp peanut sauce
- 2 tsp oyster sauce
- 1 tsp honey
- ½ cup baby cucumber, sliced

Instructions:

Hard boil the eggs. Drain and add to a cold bath. Remove the shells. Cut them in half.

Hard boil the potatoes. Peel them and cut them into wedges.

In a pan melt the butter. Add the crushed garlic and toss for 1 minute.

Add the tofu and fry until they are crispy and brown.

Transfer to a bowl. Add the cabbage, boiled potatoes, eggs, cherry tomatoes, radish and cucumber.

Add the peanut sauce, oyster sauce, honey, soy sauce, chili flakes, salt, pepper, and toss to coat everything.

Serve.

Chili Peanut Coconut Chicken

Indonesians love peanuts and they incorporate peanuts in most of their food. Their curries taste extra special because they add special ingredients like peanut paste, shrimp paste in their curries.

Serving Size: 4

Cooking Time: 30 Minutes

Ingredients:

- 4 chicken breasts cut into small pieces
- 1 tbsp ginger paste
- 2 tablespoon oil
- Fresh coriander, chopped
- 1 tsp turmeric
- 1 tbsp shrimp paste
- 1 onion, chopped
- 1 tsp paprika
- 1 dried red chili
- 2 tbsp peanut paste
- 4 cup chicken stock
- 1 cup coconut milk
- 4 cloves garlic, minced

Instructions:

In a pan, heat the oil. Fry the onion and minced garlic for 1 minute.

Add the ginger paste and shrimp paste. Toss for 1 minute.

Add the peanut paste, turmeric, and 2 tbsp of water. Cook for 1 minute.

Add the chicken and stir for 5 minutes.

Add the chicken stock and cook on high heat for 10 minutes.

Add the coconut milk, dried red chili, paprika, coriander, salt and cook for 10 minutes.

Serve hot with more coriander on top.

Indonesian Prawn Curry

Indonesians love their curries and they like it a bit spicy. Their gravy is to die for. This shrimp dish takes only 20 minutes to cook but tastes super delicious.

Serving Size: 4

Cooking Time: 20 Minutes

Ingredients:

- 1 cup deveined, peeled shrimp
- ½ cup white onion, chopped
- 1 tbsp vegetable oil
- 1 tsp garlic paste
- 1 tsp ginger paste
- ½ tsp turmeric
- 1 cup coconut milk
- 1 tsp Lemon grass, chopped
- Fresh parsley, chopped
- 1 red chili, chopped

Instructions:

In a pan add the vegetable oil. Sear the shrimp for 2 minutes.

Transfer the shrimp onto a plate.

In the pan add the onion and toss until they get caramelized.

Add the ginger paste, garlic paste, lemon grass, and toss for 2 minutes.

Add the coconut milk and then bring it to boil.

Add the seared shrimp and cook for only 5 minutes.

Serve hot with chopped red chili and parsley.

Cauliflower Curry

Cauliflower curry when cooked properly can taste better than your non-vegetarian dishes. Try this recipe and you will forget about meat.

Serving Size: 2

Cooking Time: 30 Minutes

Ingredients:

- 2 cup cauliflower florets, cut into big chunks
- 2 onion, chopped
- Fresh coriander, chopped
- 2 tomatoes, chopped
- 1 red chili, cut in half
- 1 cup vegetable stock
- Salt and pepper to taste
- ½ tsp turmeric
- 1 tbsp cashew paste
- 1 tbsp butter
- 1 tsp ginger paste
- 1 tsp garlic paste
- 1tbsp tomato sauce

Instructions:

In a wok, melt the butter. Toss the cauliflower until they get a golden color.

Transfer them onto a plate. In the wok add the onion. Toss for 1 minute.

Add the ginger paste, garlic paste, tomato sauce, turmeric, cashew paste and toss for 2 minutes.

Add the chopped tomatoes, salt, pepper, and cook for 2 minutes.

Add the stock and being it to boil. Add the cauliflower florets, red chili and cook for 10 minutes.

Add the coriander and serve hot with rice or tortilla.

Satay Chicken with Peanut Sauce

In Indonesia, this is perhaps the most popular snack or side dish out there. Both in street style and in fancy restaurant, you will find chicken satay. It is traditionally served with a peanut sauce. Check this easy and tasty peanut sauce recipe.

Serving Size: 4

Cooking Time: 25 Minutes

Ingredients:

- 1 lb. chicken thigh fillets
- 2 tbsp sweet soy sauce
- 1 tbsp butter
- 1 pinch of pepper
- 1 pinch of paprika
- 1 tbsp cooking oil
- Peanut sauce
- ½ cup peanut butter
- 2 tbsp tamari
- 1 tbsp maple syrup
- 1 tsp chili garlic sauce
- 2 tbsp lime juice
- ¼ cup water

Instructions:

First of all, combine all the peanut sauce ingredients in a bowl.

Mix until well combined. Set aside for now.

In another bowl add the chicken thigh fillets.

Add the paprika, sweet soy sauce, pepper, butter, soy sauce and coat well.

Let them marinate for 1 hour. Use wooden skewers to thread the chicken pieces.

In a grilling pan add the oil. Grill the chicken satay for 5 minutes on each side.

Serve hot with the peanut sauce.

Meatball Curry

Who does not love meatballs? In Indonesia people go one step further. They make a spicy and creamy meatball curry with an irresistible taste.

Serving Size: 4

Cooking Time: 25 Minutes

Ingredients:

- 2 cup minced meat of your choice
- 1 cup chopped shallots
- 2 tbsp oil
- Salt and pepper to taste
- 1 tsp red chili powder
- 1 dried red chili, chopped
- 1 tsp butter
- 1 cup chicken stock
- Fresh parsley, chopped
- 2 tbsp spring onion, chopped
- 1 egg
- ½ tsp turmeric
- ½ tsp cumin
- 1 tsp coriander powder
- 2 tbsp tomato sauce
- 2 tbsp soy sauce
- 2 tbsp chopped chives
- 1 tbsp honey

Instructions:

In the bowl combine the minced meat with the egg.

Add half the shallots and parsley. Mix well. Add salt and pepper.

Mix well and create meatballs.

Fry them golden brown with oil. Transfer them onto a plate.

In a large pan, melt the butter. Add the rest of the shallots.

Toss for 1 minute. Add the soy sauce, tomato sauce, turmeric, cumin, coriander powder, and toss for 1 minute.

Add the chicken stock and then bring it to boil.

Add the meatballs and cook on high heat for 5 minutes.

Add the honey, spring onion and chives on top.

Serve hot with rice.

Indonesian Stewed Beef (Rendang)

Beef stew taste quite good but this one in particular taste unforgettable. From herbs to spices, it goes so well together.

Serving Size: 4

Cooking Time: 1 hour

Ingredients:

- 2 lb. beef
- 1 tsp chili flakes
- 2 tbsp mustard oil
- ½ tsp cinnamon powder
- 5 whole cloves
- 1 tbsp ginger paste
- 1 tbsp garlic paste
- 1 pinch of nutmeg
- 6 red chilies, chopped
- 6 shallots, chopped
- 1 tsp rosemary
- Salt to taste
- 1 tsp cumin
- 1 tsp coriander powder
- 5 macadamia nuts
- 4 cup beef stock
- 1 cup yogurt

Instructions:

Cut the beef into medium chunks. Keep the bones.

In a large pot, add the mustard oil.

Sear the beef for 5 minutes. Transfer to a plate.

Add the shallots and toss for 1 minute.

Add the ginger paste, garlic paste and toss for 1 minute.

Add the cumin, coriander, salt, nutmeg whole cloves and cinnamon.

Toss for 1 minute. Add the beef stock, and then bring it to boil.

Simmer for 10 minutes. Add the beef. Cook for 20 minutes.

Add the rosemary, yogurt, macadamia nuts, red chilies, chili flakes and mix.

Cook for another 20 minutes. Serve hot.

Indonesian Coconut Rice with Grilled Chicken

Have you ever paired coconut rice with grilled chicken? It will blow your mind. Try this recipe and plunge into an Indonesian treasure.

Serving Size: 2

Cooking Time: 30 Minutes

Ingredients:

For the chicken:

- 2 chicken thighs
- Salt and pepper to taste
- 1 tbsp soy sauce
- 1 tbsp butter
- ½ tsp red chili powder

For the rice:

- 1.5 cup rice
- ½ cup grated coconut
- 1 cup coconut milk
- 2 tablespoons oil
- 1 green chili, chopped
- Fresh coriander, chopped
- 2 teaspoons salt
- 1/2 teaspoon black pepper
- 1 onion, sliced

Instructions:

Combine the salt, pepper, soy sauce and red chili powder. Marinate the chicken thighs for 30 minutes.

Add the butter on a grill. Grill the chicken thighs for 5 minutes on each side. Transfer to a serving plate.

In a pot add the rice with 3 cups of water. Bring it to boil. Cook for 5 minutes. Drain and rinse off the rice properly.

In a wok, add the oil. Fry the onion for 1 minute.

Add the grated coconut and toss for 2 minutes.

Add the cooked rice, salt, pepper, coriander, green chili, and toss for 1 minute.

Pour in the coconut milk and cook on high heat until the milk evaporates completely.

Serve hot with the grilled chicken.

Indonesian Tofu Satay

Tofu is loved by all Indonesians. Tofu Satay is similar to their chicken Satay but it caters to the vegetarians. This snack is also served with a peanut sauce. Feel free to use the peanut recipe given above.

Serving Size: 4

Cooking Time: 10 Minutes

Ingredients:

- 2 cup extra-firm tofu
- 2 tbsp flour
- 2 tbsp ginger paste
- A pinch of salt
- Pepper to taste
- 1 garlic paste
- 1/3 tsp red chili powder
- ¼ cup sweet soy sauce
- ¼ cup creamy peanut butter
- Oil for frying

Instructions:

Cut the tofu into 2 inch long and 1 inch thick tofu.

Combine the sweet soy sauce, peanut butter, red chili powder, garlic, salt, pepper, ginger and flour.

Mix well and coat the tofu in it. Let it marinate for 10 minutes.

Thread the tofu with skewers.

Fry them golden brown. Serve warm with peanut sauce.

Crispy Fried Eggs

Indonesians love eggs too. They try an incorporate egg in their lunches, snacks and breakfasts. This is a very unique fried egg recipe that tastes very good.

Serving Size: 4

Cooking Time: 20 Minutes

Ingredients:

- 4 eggs
- ½ cup flour
- 2 tbsp corn flour
- Salt to taste
- ½ tsp red chili powder
- Oil for frying

Instructions:

Boil the eggs for 5 minutes in water.

Drain and add to a bowl with cold water.

Get rid of the shells. Rub some salt and red chili powder on to the egg.

In the bowl combine the flour and corn flour. Add the salt, the red chili powder and some water to make a thick batter.

Roll the eggs into the batter and fry them golden brown for 2 minutes.

Transfer to a kitchen paper. Let them rest for 5 minutes. Cut them in half and serve warm.

Water Spinach Fry

Serving Size: 2

Cooking Time: 10 Minutes

Ingredients:

- 1.5 cup water spinach
- Salt to taste
- ½ tsp red chili powder
- 1 tsp soy sauce
- 1 tsp shrimp paste
- 4 garlic cloves, minced
- 1 red chili, chopped
- 2 tbsp oil

Instructions:

Clean the spinach and remove the stem. Dice it coarsely.

In the wok, heat the oil and add the garlic. Toss until they are golden.

Add the water spinach and cook on high heat for 2 minutes.

Add the salt, red chili powder, red chili, shrimp paste, soy sauce, and stir for 5 minutes.

Take off the heat and serve hot.

Indonesian Beef Liver

Serving Size: 4

Cooking Time: 35 Minutes

Ingredients:

- 1.5 lb. beef liver
- 1 tbsp soy sauce
- 1 tbsp smooth peanut butter
- ½ tsp sea salt
- 2 cup beef stock
- 2 white onion, cut into wedges
- 1 tsp ginger paste
- 1 tbsp garlic paste
- Fresh parsley, chopped, to serve
- 1 tbsp oil

Instructions:

Cut the beef liver into small pieces. In a pot add the liver with 2 cups of water.

Bring it to boil and drain them. Wash the liver properly.

In a large wok, heat the oil. Add the onion and toss for 1 minute.

Add the ginger paste, garlic paste, and add the boiled liver.

Add the peanut butter, soy sauce, salt, and mix well. Cook for 3 minutes.

Pour in the beef stock. Cook on high heat for 20 minutes.

Serve hot with parsley on top.

Baked Fish with Green Beans and peanuts

Serving Size: 2

Cooking Time: 20 Minutes

Ingredients:

- 1 lb. whole fish of your choice
- ½ cup peanuts
- ½ cup green beans, cut in half
- 4 garlic cloves, sliced
- 1 tbsp ginger paste
- 1 tbsp peanut butter
- 1 tsp soy sauce
- 1 tsp cumin
- 1 tbsp sugar
- 1 tbsp oil
- Salt and pepper to taste

Instructions:

Combine the soy sauce, sugar, salt, cumin, pepper, ginger paste, peanut butter and garlic.

Mix well. Marinate the fish in it for 1 hour.

Preheat the oven to 350 degrees F.

Use Aluminum foil to cover the fish with its marinated juice.

Add to a baking tray. Bake for 20 minutes.

Take it out then let it rest for 10 minutes. Remove the aluminum foil.

Serve the fish hot with the green beans and peanuts.

Spicy Egg Curry

As mentioned earlier, Indonesians love eggs. This is a spicy egg curry recipe that usually is served with rice.

Serving Size: 4

Cooking Time: 25 Minutes

Ingredients:

- 4 eggs
- 1 tbsp tamarind paste
- 1 tbsp tomato sauce
- 1 tsp chili flakes
- 1 red chili, chopped
- 1 tsp red chili powder
- 1 tsp cumin
- 1 tsp coriander powder
- 1 tbsp garlic paste
- 1 tsp ginger paste
- 1 tbsp oil
- Salt to taste
- 2 shallots, chopped
- 1 cup water
- 1 tbsp sugar

Instructions:

In a pot boil the eggs with water for only 5 minutes.

Drain well. Add cold water on top. Remove the shells.

Rub some salt onto the eggs.

In a pan add the oil and toss for shallots for 1 minute.

Add the ginger paste, garlic paste, cumin, red chili powder, salt, and mix well.

Cook for 1 minute. Add the water then bring it to boil.

Add the tamarind paste, sugar, and cook for 3 minutes.

Add the eggs and toss for 2 minutes.

Add the red chili, chili flakes and cook for 5 minutes. Serve hot.

Fish in Tamarind Sauce

Have you ever tried combining tamarind with turmeric? The gravy not only looks good but also tastes very good. The basil on top adds a lot of aroma too.

Serving Size: 2

Cooking Time: 20 Minutes

Ingredients:

- 1 large potato, peeled, sliced thinly
- 2 fish fillets
- Fresh basil leaves
- 1 tsp turmeric
- 1 tbsp tamarind paste
- 1 tsp soy sauce
- Salt to taste
- 1 tsp garlic paste
- 1 tsp red chili powder
- 1 tsp cumin
- 1 tsp sugar
- 1 tsp ginger paste
- 1 tsp coriander powder
- 2 onion, chopped
- 1 tbsp oil

Instructions:

Debone the fish. Rub some salt, turmeric and red chili powder onto the fish.

Let it marinate for 10 minutes.

In a skillet heat the oil.

Add the onion and potato. Toss for 2 minutes.

Add the garlic and ginger paste. Add the cumin, coriander powder, red chili powder, soy sauce, turmeric, and cook for 2 minutes.

Add ½ cup of water and bring it to boil.

Add the tamarind paste and the sugar. Cook for 3 minutes.

Add the fish fillets and cook for 5 minutes on high heat.

Add the fresh basil and serve hot.

Spicy Egg with Eggplant Curry

I bet you have tried egg curry before or eggplant curry before but you have never tried both combined in one curry!

Serving Size: 4

Cooking Time: 25 Minutes

Ingredients:

- 1 lb. purple eggplant
- 4 eggs
- 2 bay leaves
- 2 cardamoms
- 5 cloves
- 1 tsp sugar
- Salt to taste
- 2 tbsp tomato sauce
- 1 tbsp tamarind paste
- 3 shallots, chopped
- 1 cup water
- 1 tbsp oil
- 1 tsp red chili powder
- ½ tsp turmeric
- 1 tsp cumin
- 1 tablespoon sweet soy sauce

Instructions:

In a pot add the egg with 2 cups of water. Cook for 5 minutes.

Take off the heat. Drain and let them cool down. Remove the shells.

Cut off the stem from the eggplants. Cut them into wedges.

In a pan, heat the oil. Fry the shallots.

Add the clove, bay leaves, cardamoms and toss for 30 seconds.

Add the tamarind, tomato sauce, cumin, turmeric, red chili powder, soy sauce and cook for 5 minutes.

Add the eggplants and toss for 5 minutes.

Add the egg and toss for 2 minutes. Add the water then bring it to boil.

Simmer for 15 minutes. Serve hot.

Cassava Chips

Indonesians love cassava chips. The store bought ones are available everywhere but the homemade one is definitely better than the store bought ones. Try this recipe and enjoy.

Serving Size: 2

Cooking Time: 10 Minutes

Ingredients:

- 1 cup thinly sliced cassava
- Salt to taste
- Pepper to taste
- Oil for frying

Instructions:

In a bowl add 1 cup of water. Add the cassava slices and let them soak for 30 minutes.

Drain and rinse off properly.

In a deep fryer, heat the oil.

Add the cassava chips and cook until they are crispy.

Add the salt and pepper on top before serving.

Spicy Tempeh Fries

To express Indonesian's love for vegan food, they try to incorporate tofu and tempeh in their food quite often. This tempeh recipe is spicy and crispy.

Serving Size: 2

Cooking Time: 10 Minutes

Ingredients:

- 1 cup tempeh
- 2 red chilies, chopped
- 2 tbsp sweet soy sauce
- A pinch of salt
- A pinch of pepper
- A pinch of red chili powder

Instructions:

Cut the tempeh in thin slices.

Coat the tempeh with salt, pepper, red chili powder, and mix well.

In a wok, melt the butter.

Add the tempeh and toss for 2 minutes.

Add the soy sauce, red chili and toss for 5 minutes.

Serve hot.

Sesame Balls

When it comes to desserts, Indonesians have quite some interesting desserts that make them unique. This sesame ball recipe is simple and very delicious.

Serving Size: 6

Cooking Time: 25 Minutes

Ingredients:

- 2 ½ slabs brown candy, chopped
- 3 cup glutinous rice flour
- A pinch of salt
- 1/3 cup white sesame seeds
- 1 cup of sweetened red bean paste, homemade
- 2 quarts of vegetable oil

Instructions:

1. In the large mixing bowl, combine the chopped slabs brown candy.

2. Melt them. Add the rice flour, salt and red bean paste. Mix well.

3. Use your hands to make round small balls.

4. Roll them onto the sesame seeds.

5. Fry them golden brown with vegetable oil.

6. Let them rest for 30 minutes.

7. Serve in room temperature.

Indonesian Spice Cake

Serving Size: 4

Cooking Time: 25 Minutes

Ingredients:

- 2 cup cake flour
- 1 tsp baking powder
- 1 pinch of clove
- 1 pinch of nutmeg
- 1 tsp vanilla extract
- 1 pinch of cinnamon
- 1.5 cup sugar
- 2 egg yolks
- 4 eggs
- 1 cup butter

Instructions:

Preheat an oven to 350 degrees F. Add parchment paper on the bottom of the cake pan.

Shift the dry ingredients in a bowl.

In another bowl, whisk the eggs for 3 minutes. Add the egg yolk and mix well.

Add the sugar then beat for 2 minutes.

Add the butter, vanilla and beat for 2 minutes.

Add the dry ingredients and fold them in.

Pour into the cake pan. Bake for 1 hour.

Let them rest for 20 minutes. Take the cake out and remove the parchment paper.

Cut into slices and serve.

Nagasari or Stuffed Rice Cake

Among all the desserts of Indonesia, I found this one quite unique. It is wrapped with banana leaf and then stemmed. The ingredients used are commonly found anywhere in the world, so anyone can make it.

Serving Size: 12 pieces

Cooking Time: 25 Minutes

Ingredients:

- 1 cup coconut milk
- ½ cup rice flour
- 2 tbsp tapioca starch
- 2 tablespoon water
- ½ cup sugar
- ½ teaspoon salt
- 2 bananas, sliced
- 1 large banana leaf

Instructions

Cut the banana leaf into 12 pieces.

Combine the rice flour, tapioca starch, salt, sugar, and coconut milk.

Add the water and mix well. Knead well and divide the dough into 12 balls.

Roll them out and add one banana slice inside one sheet. Roll them tightly.

Wrap the banana leaves on them tightly. Repeat with all the ingredients.

Stem them for 20 minutes. Let them rest for 20 minutes. Serve cold.

Wingko Babat or Coconut Pancake

Coconut is a super food. Indonesians love it and this coconut pancake tastes quite good.

Serving Size: 4

Cooking Time: 25 Minutes

Ingredients:

- 1 cup grated coconut meat
- 1 cup sugar
- 1.5 cup rice flour
- A pinch of salt
- 1 cup coconut milk
- 1 egg
- 1 tsp coconut oil
- 1 drop of vanilla extract
- 1 tbsp sesame seeds

Instructions:

Whisk the egg. Add the coconut oil and mix.

Add the sugar, salt and mix well. Add the grated coconut, coconut milk, rice flour and vanilla.

Mix well and create a semi smooth batter. Add the sesame seeds and mix.

Fry them golden brown in batches. Serve them in room temperature.

Kolak Pisang

This is such a creamy, milky dessert with fruits that tastes really refreshing. You can make a big batch and enjoy this dessert for 3 days in the fridge.

Serving Size: 4

Cooking Time: 25 Minutes

Ingredients:

Instructions:

- 4 cup coconut milk
- 1 cup palm sugar, grated
- ½ cup sugar
- 1 tsp vanilla powder
- 4 tbsp custard powder
- 2 pandan leaves, chopped
- 2 bananas, sliced
- 2 mangos, cubed
- 1 teaspoon of salt

Instructions:

In a pot add the coconut milk with palm sugar.

Add the sugar and mix well. Cook for 4 minutes.

Add the vanilla powder, custard powder, pandan leaves and salt.

Cook for 5 minutes. Drain the mixture. Discard the pandan leaves.

Let the mixture cool down for 30 minutes.

Add the sliced banana and mango. Fold in gently. Serve cold.

Vegetable Fritters

This is a classic Indonesian snack recipe with lots of vegetables. It has all the right herbs and spices. You can feel free to add any vegetable of your choice in this recipe

Serving Size: 2

Cooking Time: 10 Minutes

Ingredients:

- 1 cup rice flour
- ½ cup grated zucchini
- ½ cup grated potatoes
- ½ cup gram flour
- ½ tsp salt
- ½ tsp garlic powder
- ½ tsp cumin
- 1 egg
- ½ tsp red chili powder
- Oil for frying

Instructions:

Combine the rice flour, gram flour, salt, garlic, cumin and red chili powder.

Add the egg and beat well.

Add in the vegetables and mix well. Add some water to make a semi tight batter.

In a pan add the oil and fry the fritters golden brown.

Serve warm.

Conclusion

Indonesian cuisine is diversified with many ingredients and flavors. They love food in general and it is evident in their cooking. The care they take to cook any dish is a proof of their love for good food. Homemade food always tastes better and costs much less. The ingredients they use are fresh. Most large super shops contain a section of different countries grocery's, so try looking for their unique ingredients in your local shop and try these authentic Indonesian food.

About the Author

Born in New Germantown, Pennsylvania, Stephanie Sharp received a Masters degree from Penn State in English Literature. Driven by her passion to create culinary masterpieces, she applied and was accepted to The International Culinary School of the Art Institute where she excelled in French cuisine. She has married her cooking skills with an aptitude for business by opening her own small cooking school where she teaches students of all ages.

Stephanie's talents extend to being an author as well and she has written over 400 e-books on the art of cooking and baking that include her most popular recipes.

Sharp has been fortunate enough to raise a family near her hometown in Pennsylvania where she, her husband and children live in a beautiful rustic house on an extensive piece of land. Her other passion is taking care of the furry members of her family which include 3 cats, 2 dogs and a potbelly pig named Wilbur.

Watch for more amazing books by Stephanie Sharp coming out in the next few months.

Author's Afterthoughts

I am truly grateful to you for taking the time to read my book. I cherish all of my readers! Thanks ever so much to each of my cherished readers for investing the time to read this book!

With so many options available to you, your choice to buy my book is an honour, so my heartfelt thanks at reading it from beginning to end!

I value your feedback, so please take a moment to submit an honest and open review on Amazon so I can get valuable insight into my readers' opinions and others can benefit from your experience.

Thank you for taking the time to review!

Stephanie   **Sharp**

For announcements about new releases, please

follow my author page on Amazon.com!

You can find that at:

https://www.amazon.com/author/stephanie-sharp

*or Scan **QR-code** below.*

Printed in Great Britain
by Amazon

85662804R00055